JK's
Quick Start Guide
to
Amazon Ads Marketing

Other books in JK's Self-Publishing Guides:

EBooks

JK's Quick Start Guide to Scrivener (Mac)

JK's Quick Start Guide to Scrivener (Windows)

JK's Quick Start Guide to Publishing Books on Amazon KDP

JK's Quick Start Guide to Publishing Books on Ingram Spark

JK's Quick Start Guide to Copyrighting Your Book

Paperback

JK's Quick Start Guide to Scrivener (Mac)

JK's
Quick Start Guide
to Amazon Ads
Marketing

JK Lincoln

ISBN 978-1-938322-60-0

Ralston Store Publishing
P.O. Box 1684
Prescott, Arizona 86302

Table of Contents

1. The best way to access your Amazon Ads account is to click Bookshelf at the top of your Amazon KDP Account page.

2A. The next step depends on how you've set up your book. If it is in Select like the first novel in my cozy mystery series, it will look like this. Click on *Promote and Advertise.* (If you click on the ellipsis, you will get a menu where you have another chance to click *Promote and Advertise.*)

2B. If your book is not in Select, then it will look like this. Click on the ellipsis.

2C. Then this little box will pop up. Click on *Promote and Advertise.*

2D. The above three pictures all refer to eBooks. If you have a paperback, the procedure is the same. Click on *Promote and Advertise.*

3. The top arrow will show the title of the book that you chose to promote. Second arrow is whether or not you've chosen to participate in the KDP Select program. On this book, I have. Third arrow down on the left points to Kindle Countdown Deal and Free Book Promotion. [Brief description of Kindle Countdown Deal and Free Book Promotion. Countdown: your book is for sale for $5. On the first day of Countdown, you lower the price to $2, second day, it is $3, third day, it is $4, and on the fifth day, it returns to $5. You can set the increments and set how many days. Free Book: You can set your book for free for three to five days. Both promotions have eligibility requirements. Click *Learn More* on each one to learn more.] **If you are advertising a paperback, the Select part and the Kindle Countdown and Free Book Promotion will not show up.** The horizontal arrow on the right points to choosing a marketplace. I will cover the other markets later, but for now, choose Amazon.com. And then the vertical arrow points to *Create an ad campaign*. Click it!

Secrets for Sale

Promote your book on Amazon

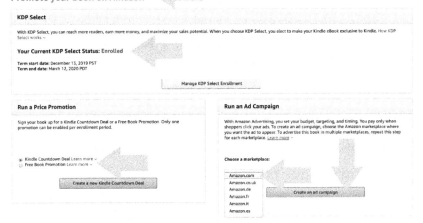

KDP Select

With KDP Select, you can reach more readers, earn more money, and maximize your sales potential. When you choose KDP Select, you elect to make your Kindle eBook exclusive to Kindle. How KDP Select works ⌄

Your Current KDP Select Status: Enrolled

Term start date: December 13, 2019 PST
Term end date: March 12, 2020 PDT

Manage KDP Select Enrollment

Run a Price Promotion

Sign your book up for a Kindle Countdown Deal or a Free Book Promotion. Only one promotion can be enabled per enrollment period.

○ Kindle Countdown Deal Learn more ⌄
○ Free Book Promotion Learn more ⌄

Create a new Kindle Countdown Deal

Run an Ad Campaign

With Amazon Advertising, you set your budget, targeting, and timing. You pay only when shoppers click your ads. To create an ad campaign, choose the Amazon marketplace where you want the ad to appear. To advertise this book in multiple marketplaces, repeat this step for each marketplace. Learn more ⌄

Choose a marketplace:

Amazon.com
Amazon.co.uk
Amazon.de
Amazon.fr
Amazon.it
Amazon.es

Create an ad campaign

4. Choose the one on the left, Sponsored Products. Click *Continue*. Lockscreen Ads are the ones you use that pop up on a Kindle device before it is unlocked. Lockscreen ads are a whole 'nother story and will not be covered in this book.

Choose your campaign type

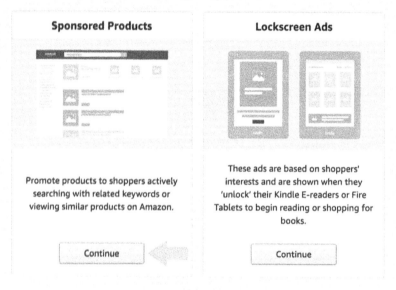

Sponsored Products

Promote products to shoppers actively searching with related keywords or viewing similar products on Amazon.

Continue

Lockscreen Ads

These ads are based on shoppers' interests and are shown when they 'unlock' their Kindle E-readers or Fire Tablets to begin reading or shopping for books.

Continue

5. Enter the name for your campaign. The space will already have something in it . . . Just type over it. Might as well start the campaign today! What are you waiting for? Generally, I never put in an end date. If you want to stop the ad later, you can do that. I always start with a dollar which is the minimum. You can raise the limit later. Often, I get emails that my daily budget is spent and I should raise the limit. I usually ignore them. The budget resets at the end of the day. Choose *Manual Targeting*, because that's where the power of Amazon Ads are. See the little "i" in a gray circle by each entry? If you run your mouse over that, (no need to click), it will give you more information. For example, the "i" next to the daily budget will tell you that it can charge you 10% more on any given day, but at the end of the month, you will not be charged for more than days x daily budget.

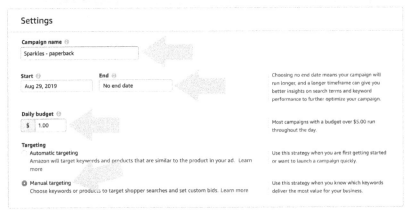

6A. This part is a little complicated. My first arrow points to blue text that says *Learn More*. And all three choices (*Dynamic - down only, Dynamic - up and down, and Fixed Bids*) have *Learn More*. Click there for more information on each of them. I'm only giving you the bare bones explanation. *Dynamic bids - down only*: If you bid $0.50 for an ad, and Amazon thinks you would still win by going down, you might end up paying $0.45 or even $0.30 for it. All of my ads are *down only*. *Dynamic bids - up and down*: By Amazon's discretion (their algorithms), they will raise or lower your bid as they see fit. So if you bid $0.50 for an ad, you might end up paying $1.00. With Amazon doing that, you may end up with a sale, where you might not have if they would have left it $0.50. *Fixed Bids*: As it says, your bid will remain fixed no matter what. If you bid $0.50, it will always be $0.50. Make your choice.

Campaign bidding strategy ⓘ

◉ **Dynamic bids - down only**
We'll lower your bids in real time when your ad may be less likely to convert   sale. Any campaign created before April 22, 2019 used this setting. Learn more

○ **Dynamic bids - up and down**
We'll raise your bids (by a maximum of 100%) in real time when your ad may be more likely to convert to a sale, and lower your bids when less likely to convert to a sale. Learn more

○ **Fixed bids**
We'll use your exact bid and any manual adjustments you set, and won't change your bids based on likelihood of a sale. Learn more

∧ Adjust bids by placement (replaces Bid+) ⓘ
In addition to your bidding strategy, you can increase bids by up to 900%. Learn more

Top of search (first page) | 0 | % | Example: A $0.75 bid will remain $0.75 for this place   nt.

Product pages | 0 | % | Example: A $0.75 bid will remain $0.75 for this placement.

6B. If you click *Adjust bids by placement*, it opens up another option. I have entered 10(%) on the first one and 100(%) on the second so you can see how it works. Again, if you click *Learn More*, you will get a lot more information. On the first one labeled *Top of search*, I entered 10%. Their example shows how that would affect the bid. 10% would raise a $0.75 bid to $0.83 to go to the top of the search. On the second one labeled *Product Pages*, I entered 100%. Their example shows that it would raise a $0.75 bid to $1.50. This part is completely optional. Enter something or don't. Your choice.

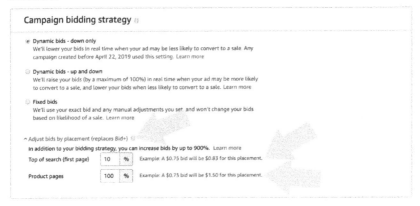

7. *Custom text*! That is where the <very abbreviated> blurb will go. (Later in the process.)

8. If you see your book on the right-hand side, proceed to 9. Otherwise, find your book on the left where there will be a listing of all your books. Click where it says *Add,* and the chosen book will appear on the right. You can see on the left where my book now says *Added.*

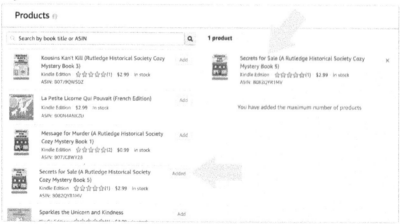

9. Choose *Keyword targeting*. Keywords are the power of these ads.

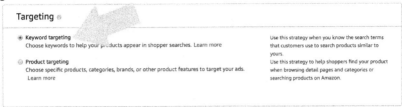

10A. *Keyword targeting* is next. Click the dropdown box where it says *Suggested bid*.

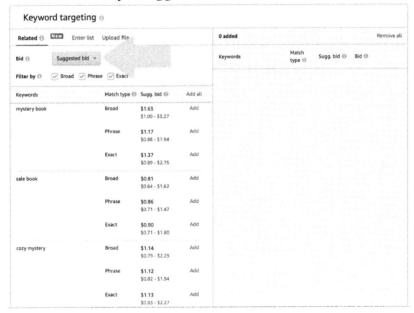

10B. Choose *Custom bid.*

Keyword targeting ⓘ

Related ⓘ NEW Enter list Upload file				0 added				Remove all
				Keywords	Match type ⓘ	Sugg. bid ⓘ	Bid ⓘ	

Bid ⓘ

Suggested bid
Uses past bidding activity to predict bids that are more likely to win
Custom bid
Can customize bids for each keyword
Default bid
Links multiple keywords to the same bid value

Filter by ⓘ

Keywords

mystery book			Add
	Phrase	$1.17 $0.88 - $1.94	Add
	Exact	$1.37 $0.89 - $2.75	Add
sale book	Broad	$0.81 $0.64 - $1.62	Add
	Phrase	$0.86 $0.71 - $1.47	Add
	Exact	$0.90 $0.71 - $1.80	Add
cozy mystery	Broad	$1.14 $0.79 - $2.29	Add
	Phrase	$1.12 $0.82 - $1.94	Add
	Exact	$1.13 $0.83 - $2.27	Add

10C. After you choose *Custom Bid*, this will pop up next on the upper left of your screen. The first arrow points to what popped up for me: $0.82 as a suggested bid. The following day, the second arrow points to $0.93 as the suggested bid. For the same book! It went up more than ten cents in one day! And the third arrow points to $0.25, which is the bid that I chose. You can change that bid to anything you want. It's a "custom bid" and it is your choice.

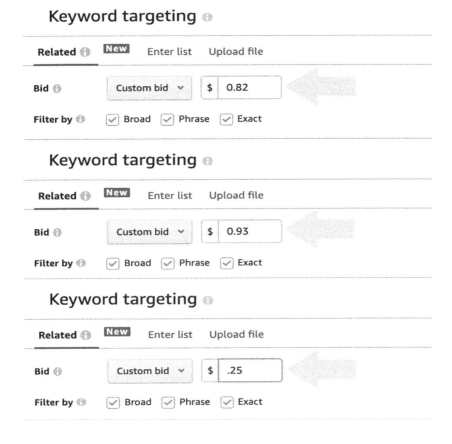

10D. Still at the top left, the arrow points to the little "i" by *Filter by.*

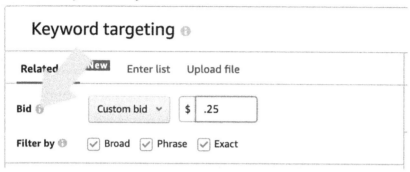

And if you click that "i" you will get a clear explanation of the terms *broad, phrase,* and *exact.*

Match types allow you to fine-tune which customer search terms trigger your ads.

Broad: Contains all the keywords in any order and includes plurals, variations and related keywords.

Phrase: Contains the exact phrase or sequence of keywords.

Exact: Exactly matches the keyword or sequence of keywords.

Filter by ❶ ☑ Broad ☑ Phrase ☑ Exact

10E. Now look at the three vertical arrows. They point to *mystery book, sale book, cozy mystery.* Amazon generates these words/phrases from the information about your book. My book, called Secrets for Sale, has nothing to do with "sale book." So that is one of their suggestions I will not use. I will use mystery book and cozy mystery. There are a ton more words and phrases that they've generated, and I'll probably use most of them, plus add some of my own. Unless someone clicks on them, they won't cost anything. And now that you know what *Broad, Phrase,* and *Exact* means, make your choice with the arrows on the right

10F. Remember I set up my daily budget as $1.00? This is what it looks like when I accept *Suggested bid* instead of changing it to *Custom bid*. The suggested bids go above my daily budget.

The way I fixed it was to change *Suggested bid* to *Custom bid* and then *Remove all* the keywords that I had added. I could also have changed the bid amounts individually, but if I had added a lot of keywords, that would take longer than removing and then re-adding them correctly.

10G. Okay, we have a Custom bid of $0.25 on the left, and on the right, you can see that the Suggested bid and my bid are not even close. That means I may not get any impressions, or it could mean that the impressions I do get will be a lot cheaper than what they recommend.

10H. This is an advance option if you have a list of keywords in a separate file.

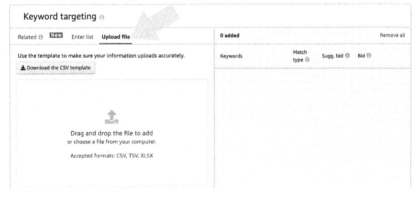

10I. Click *Enter list* at the top. It will open that little box on the left, so you can enter other keywords. As I was adding women sleuths, an even smaller box on the bottom opened to show me other similar words. You can choose to add them by clicking *Add all keywords in this list*. If it's a long list and most of them are relevant and one or two are not, add them all and then get rid of the ones that aren't. See my original keywords on the right-hand side? To the very right side you will see an *x*. If you click that, it will delete them. Many of the words you type in will open up another box either above or below. Check them out, because they might give you new ideas. When you have all your keywords that you can think of (the more the better), then click on *Add keywords* (lower center arrow) to move them to the right portion of the window.

10J. After you click the *Add keywords* button, it will look like this. The left arrow points to how many keywords you added. (You should try for at least 100. The more the better.) My two right-hand arrows point to one of my favorite mystery writers, JA Jance, and one of her characters, Joanna Brady. You can put authors, characters, book titles, and series titles in your keyword list. Use your imagination. This is the magic of Amazon ads, because you can't do that when you enter your seven keywords as you are publishing. But here you can, and it's perfectly acceptable in Amazon's Terms of Service. You can add up to 1000 words. If you can't think of them now, add more later.

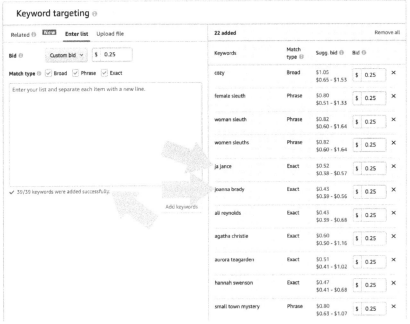

11. Now we come to *Negative keywords*. I have a seven book *sweet* romance series. Sweet means clean, no sex. So if *romance* was one of my keywords, then I would get a lot of clicks from people who had no interest in clean romance. So to stop at least some of that, I would put a negative keyword of *steamy*. So any time someone searched for steamy romance, my books would not appear. If I didn't have the negative keyword *steamy*, then off my broad designation of romance, my books would have appeared. Another way to use negative keywords is after your ad has run for a while. If you notice you're getting a lot of clicks on a word that's not producing any sales, you might want to include that or a qualifier in the negative keywords.

12. The *Creative* box is where you put your mini-blurb. The top arrow points to the *Custom Text* box. You are allowed 150 characters. It's not much, so use them well! The second arrow will point to a picture of your book cover. The bottom arrow points to the text that you typed into the *Custom Text* box. It will appear as you type, so you can see what it will look like. CAUTION! You cannot change the blurb later.

13A. You will find this just beneath the *Creative* box. If you're not ready to launch your advertising campaign yet, at least click *Save as draft* to save it. If you've already saved, then instead of *Save as draft*, you will see *Saved*. In case you're having second thoughts about the whole idea, let me ease your mind. AMAZON ADS ARE *PAY-PER-CLICK*. That means that you can have 1000 *impressions* of your ad, and unless someone clicks on one of them, you haven't spent a dime. You only pay when someone clicks on your ad. And the cost will not go above the daily budget that you set earlier. And I'm about to show you how you can check to see how many impressions, how many clicks, and what you've spent so far. Before your ad goes live, Amazon has to approve it. They will send you an email when it's approved or rejected.

Save as draft	Launch campaign

13B. At the top right-hand corner of your screen, this is another option. And again, if you have already saved, then instead of *Save as draft*, it will say *Saved*.

14. This confirms that you created your *campaign* (ad). Now is your chance to review it, and you may edit it if you wish. Hooray! You did it! You will receive an email saying that they will evaluate your ad, and then within three days, usually less, they will send another email saying they accept or reject it. Most of the reasons it won't approve your ad is because of the cover: guns in certain positions, blood, too explicit. I've had two rejected—one because of blood on the cover and another because it was in Spanish. Good luck! Click *Edit* if you want to change anything, otherwise, click *Go to campaign manager*. If you click *Edit* and make changes (or not), then click *Go to Campaign manager*.

✓ Congratulations, you successfully created your campaign.
Note: your campaign is pending approval from our moderation team. Moderation may take up to 72 hours and we will notify you when it has been approved.

[Go to campaign manager] [Edit campaign]

Review your campaign

Campaign name	Secrets for Sale
Portfolio	
Schedule	Jan 22, 2020 - No end date
Daily budget	$1.00
Targeting	Manual targeting
Ad format	Custom text ad
Products	1
Keywords	26
Negative keywords	0
Campaign bidding strategy	Dynamic bids - down only
Adjust bids by placement	Top of search (first page): 0% Product pages: 0%

15A. This is the top part of the *Campaign Manager* screen. Let me break it down for you. (And even if it says *Delivering*, it still has to go through the review process first.) You will receive an email when it passes the review phase.

15B. When you run your mouse over those three lines in the upper left-hand corner,

this will pop up. If you click *Campaigns*, it will take you back to the previous screen. When you click *Reports*, another screen comes up.

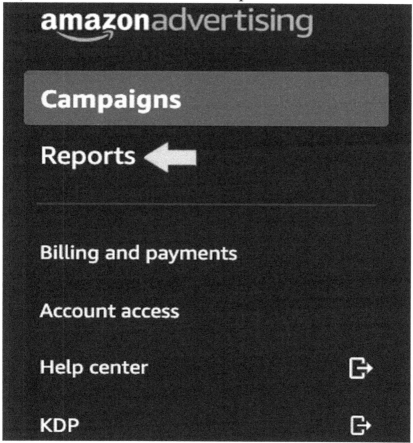

16. On the upper left-hand side of your screen, click *Create report*. If you've already run any and want to look for it, type in the name in the right hand box.

17A. If you click *Search term*, then the box on the right opens, and you can choose any of those reports. *Time unit* choice is *Summary* or *Daily*. The *Report period* has several choices and a calendar pops up to help you with your choice.

17B. You can name it anything you want (top arrow). For *Delivery,* you can choose *Now, Future,* or *Recurring.* Now is—now.

Future is anytime in the future. Double click in the box and a calendar pops up for you.

Schedule the *Frequency* (*Daily, Weekly, Monthly*) and then double click in the *End date* box to specify an end date.

17C. On the upper right-hand side of the screen, click *Run report*.

17D. You'll see this confirmation page next.

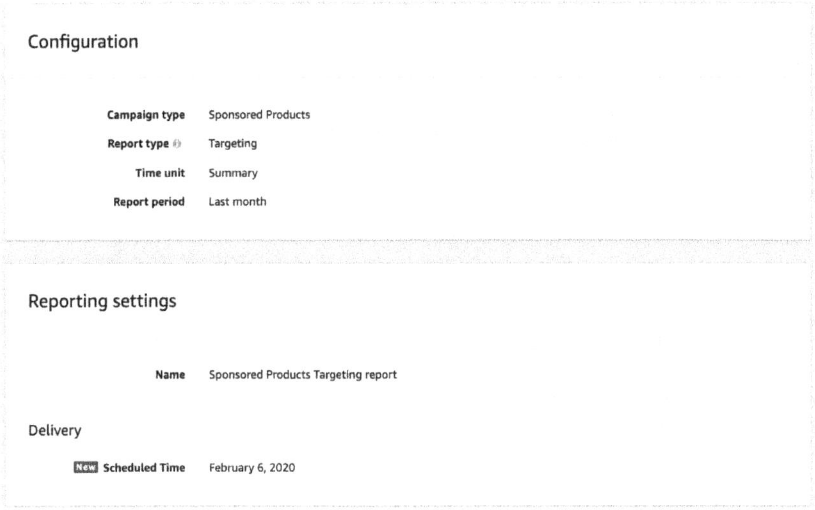

Configuration

Campaign type	Sponsored Products
Report type ⓘ	Targeting
Time unit	Summary
Report period	Last month

Reporting settings

Name	Sponsored Products Targeting report

Delivery

New **Scheduled Time**	February 6, 2020

17E. In the upper left-hand corner, click *Reports*.

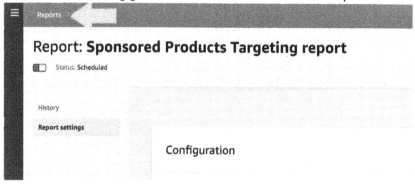

18. Click on the icon where the left arrow is pointing. If you click the blue report name where the right arrow is pointing, then you will get . . .

. . . this screen, and you still have to click the icon under *Download*!

19A. From the *Reports* page, run your mouse over the three lines in the upper left-hand corner and click Billing and Payments.

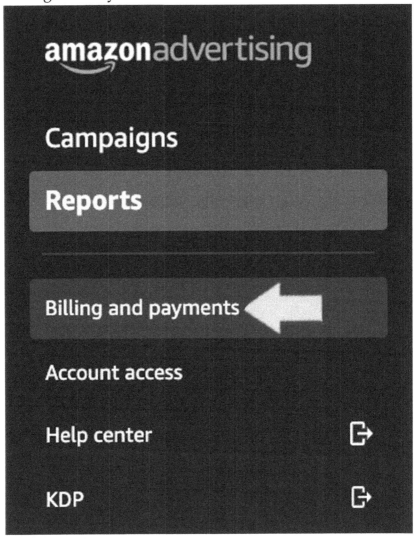

19B. This is the top portion of the next screen you see. Beneath it are past payments.

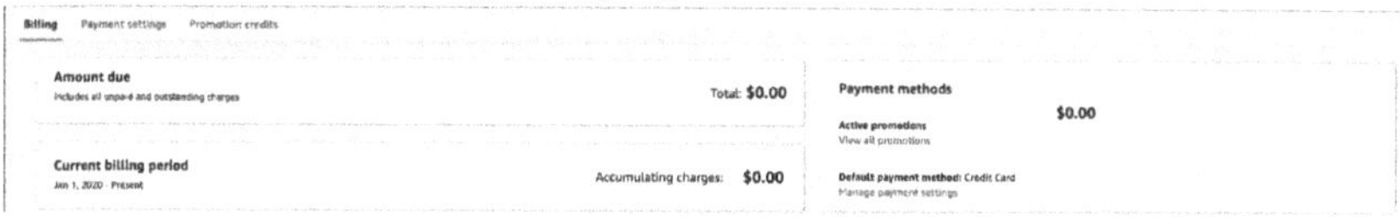

19C. This is the left side of your screen. The first arrow points to *Billing,* which is what we're looking at now. The other two arrows point to the *Amount due* and the *Current billing* period.

19D. View all promotions shows if you have any *Countdown* deals or other *promotion*. It does not show your *ads*. *Manage payment settings* is for your credit card to pay for the ads.

19E. Back to the upper left-hand corner. Click on *Payment settings* for *Account information* and *Account details*. This screen will come up next.

19F. Click *Promotion Credits* to get this screen. Various items about promotions (not ads): *Summary, Promo codes, Promotion credit offers,* and *Redeemed promotions.*

19G. Move your mouse to the lines in the upper left-hand corner again and then click *Account access*. It will just give you information on your account like your email address and your *Role*. Mine is *Admin*, because it's my account. It will also give you the option of adding someone else to your account by clicking *Invite user*.

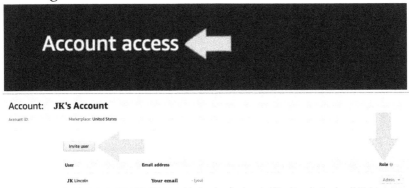

19H. If you click *Help center*, it takes you to Amazon's help pages. If you click KDP, it takes you to the KDP sign-in page. (It seems to do that even if you're already signed in.)

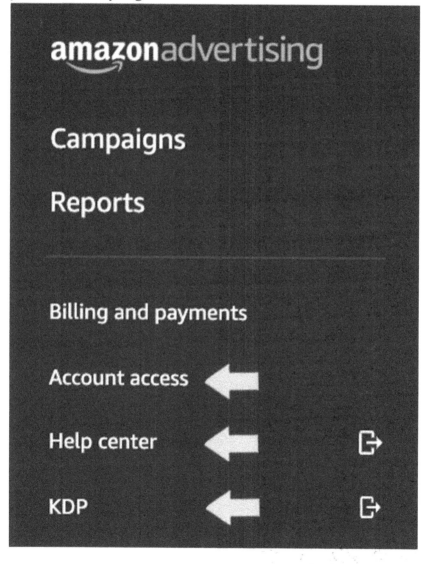

20A. Use the three lines on the upper left to get back to *Campaigns*. Create campaign only works for a new campaign in the US. If you want to create one for another country, you need to go back to your KDP bookshelf and follow the instructions from #1. The second arrow with the dropdown list was from the option *Filter by*. It gives you lots of choices. The third arrow points to *Show chart*. If you click that, it will show you a cool graph. (Then you need to click *Hide chart* to get rid of it!) If you click the date range, a calendar will pop up that you can adjust. *Export* creates a report in *csv* format. (*Comma separated values, which can be opened with a program that creates spreadsheets.*)

20B. Here's a shortcut back to your KDP account. Using the three line menu in the upper left corner, click Help center and then click Bookshelf on the top menu. Find your book that you want to advertise on a foreign market and click *Promote and Advertise* or the ellipsis to get to the menu with Promote and Advertise (that's if your book is in Select.)

21. You'll recognize this screen from our first time through. But this time, we will click the dropdown box where it says *Choose,* and then choose the country we want to advertise in. (UK=United Kingdom, de=Germany, fr=France, it=Italy, and es=Spain.) I'm choosing Spain. Top arrow points to the title of your book. Click on *Amazon.es* and then click *Create an ad campaign.*

El Pequeño Unicornio que Pudo
Promote your book on Amazon

KDP Select

With KDP Select, you can reach more readers, earn more money, and maximize your sales potential. When you choose KDP Select, you elect to make your Kindle eBook exclusive to Kindle. How KDP Select works

Enroll in KDP Select

Run a Price Promotion

Sign your book up for a Kindle Countdown Deal or a Free Book Promotion. Only one promotion can be enabled per enrollment period.

Kindle Countdown Deal Learn more
Free Book Promotion Learn more

Your book must be enrolled in KDP Select to run a price promotion.

Run an Ad Campaign

With Amazon Advertising, you set your budget, targeting, and timing. You pay only when shoppers click your ads. To create an ad campaign, choose the Amazon marketplace where you want the ad to appear. To advertise this book in multiple marketplaces, repeat this step for each marketplace. Learn more

Choose a marketplace:

Amazon.com
Amazon.co.uk
Amazon.de
Amazon.fr
Amazon.it
Amazon.es

Create an ad campaign

22A. This isn't going to work! Let's fix it.

Selecciona el tipo de campaña

Sponsored Products

Promociona productos a los compradores que buscan activamente con palabras clave relacionadas o visitan productos similares en Amazon.

Continuar

22B. In the upper right-hand corner, click your name (the one next to the bell), and this will pop up. Change it to *English* so we can proceed.

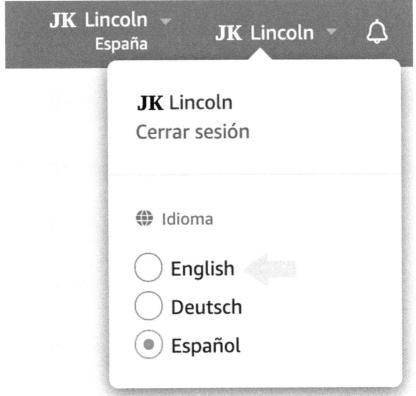

22C. That's better. Now click *Continue*.

Choose your campaign type

Sponsored Products

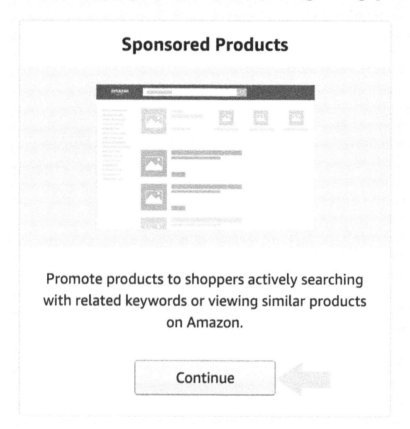

Promote products to shoppers actively searching with related keywords or viewing similar products on Amazon.

Continue

23.This will be at the top of your screen. It needs to be done, but it's easier to save it for later.

24. These are the same as we did on the Amazon.com book. The reason I added "Spain" to the *Campaign name* is because when I receive a *"Your campaign(s) are reaching or have reached budgets"* email from Amazon, I want to know which market it is from.

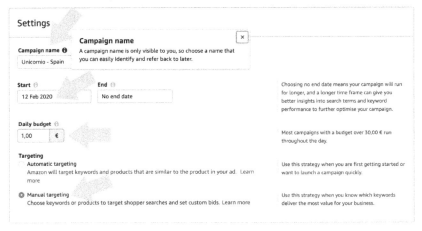

25. This is the same as Amazon.com.

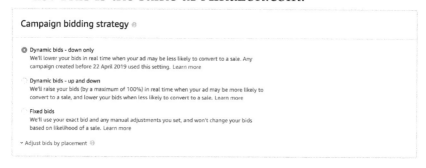

26. This is something different. It groups ads together. I usually leave it the way it is. Feel free to name it.

Create an ad group

An ad group is a group of ads sharing the same set of keywords and products. Consider grouping products that fall within the same category and price point range. You can edit your campaign after launch to create additional ad groups in campaign manager. Learn more

Settings

Ad group name ⓘ New

Ad group 1

27. Your book should come up on the right automagically. If it doesn't, click *Add* to get it there.

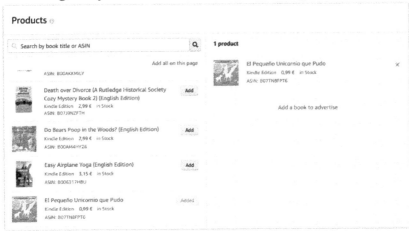

28. Choose *Keyword targeting* as we did before.

29A. Change the bid to *Custom bid* and change the bid amount. Remember that it is euros! Do a search on euros to dollars to see how much you'd like to spend. *Today*, 0,14 is about $0.15.

29B. Click *Enter list*, type in all your words—as many as you can think of—(you might get more ideas from the ones that pop up as you type), and then click *Add keywords* at the bottom.

29C. These are some of the words and phrases that popped up for me when I typed in unicornio. There is an option to *Add all keywords in this list*, but several of them were inappropriate, so I didn't do that.

Targeting 🔍

unicornio toys

unicornio

unicornio peluche

unicornios para niñas

unicornio party supplies birthday

unicornio party

unicornio backpack

unicornio inflable

unicornio backdrop

unicornio accesorios para niñas

Add all keywords in this list

This list includes search terms that shoppers use.

unicornio party
unicornio accesorios para niñas
unicornios para niñas
unicornio

29D. On the right-hand side, click the *x* on all the ones that you don't want.

15 added				Remove all
Keywords	Match type ⓘ	Sugg. bid ⓘ Apply all	Bid ⓘ	
unicornio party	Broad	0,42 € 0,30 € - 0,76 €	0,14 €	✕
unicornio party	Phrase	0,76 € 0,37 € - 1,52 €	0,14 €	✕
unicornio party	Exact	0,76 € 0,42 € - 1,52 €	0,14 €	✕
unicornio accesorios para niñas	Broad	0,39 € 0,24 € - 0,39 €	0,14 €	✕
unicornio accesorios para niñas	Phrase	-	0,14 €	✕
unicornio accesorios para niñas	Exact	-	0,14 €	✕
unicornios para niñas	Broad	0,56 € 0,31 € - 0,98 €	0,14 €	✕
unicornios para niñas	Phrase	0,50 € 0,32 € - 0,91 €	0,14 €	✕
unicornios para niñas	Exact	0,56 € 0,44 € - 1,12 €	0,14 €	✕
unicornio peluche	Broad	0,46 € 0,25 € - 0,91 €	0,14 €	✕

30. Negative keywords again. Make your choice.

31. Make sure you click *Save as draft*. (It will say *Saved*, if you've already saved it.) It will not allow you to Launch campaign until you've set up your payment information.

32. Click *Update your payment settings*.

⚠ You cannot launch a campaign due to an issue with your payment method. You may only save a draft of your new campaign.
Update your payment settings to launch your campaign.
Reference: 260-3183954-2025632

33. Click *Credit or debit card* if it's not already clicked and then click *Continue*.

Set up your payment settings

Set up your payment method and your account details to begin advertising. Learn more ☑

Choose a payment method

⊙ **Credit or debit card**
Advertising costs will be charged to your selected credit or debit card when you reach your spend limit or at end of the month.

Continue

34. Check *Advertiser/Brand* owner unless you're an agency.

Set up your payment settings

Set up your payment method and your account details to begin advertising. Learn more ☑

Set up your account details

Account manager

Account manager identification

⊙ Advertiser/Brand owner
Advertisers create and manage advertising for your own products or products that you sell.

◯ Agency
Agencies manage advertising on behalf of one or more organisations that sells products on Amazon.

Advertiser name (required)

35. Fill in your name and your VAT number if you have one. If you don't, it's okay.

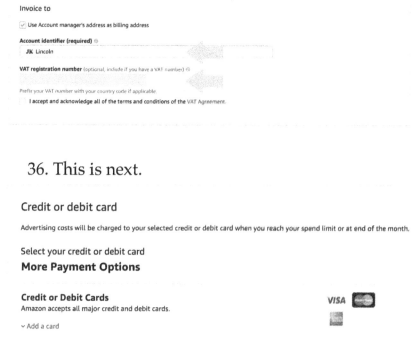

Invoice to

☑ Use Account manager's address as billing address

Account identifier (required) ⊕

JK Lincoln

VAT registration number (optional, include if you have a VAT number) ⊕

Prefix your VAT number with your country code if applicable.

☐ I accept and acknowledge all of the terms and conditions of the VAT Agreement.

36. This is next.

Credit or debit card

Advertising costs will be charged to your selected credit or debit card when you reach your spend limit or at end of the month.

Select your credit or debit card
More Payment Options

Credit or Debit Cards
Amazon accepts all major credit and debit cards.

⌄ Add a card

VISA

37. Click *Save payment method* to save.

Back to payment method selection   **Save payment method**

38. Move your mouse over the lines in the upper left-hand corner, and when this pops up, click on *Campaigns*.

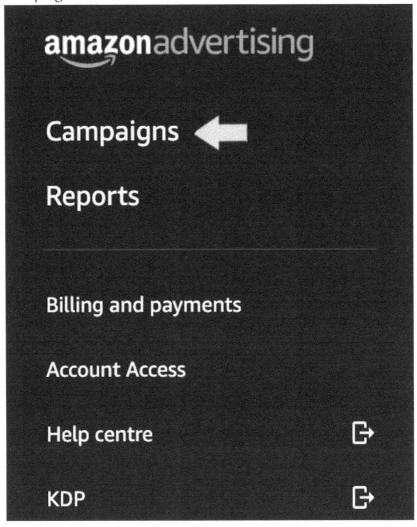

39. In the upper left-hand corner, click Drafts.

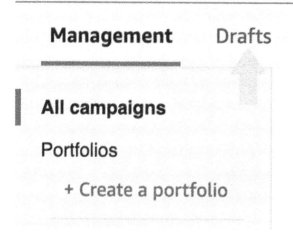

And this comes up next:

40. Now click *Edit,* and you'll have your ad back. Check it over and make sure that everything is correct, and then click *Launch Campaign* at the bottom (or the top.)

Type	Status	Actions
Sponsored Products	Draft	Edit Delete

Congratulations! You've done it! You will receive an email saying that they will evaluate your ad, and then within three days, usually less, they will send another email saying they accept or reject it.

Author's Note

If you have any questions or comments about one of my Quick Start Guides, please ask or comment on my blog:

https://self-publisherquickstartblog.blogspot.com.

Also, write in if you have any requests for a new Quick Start Guide. Thank you!

If this book helped you and you liked it, please leave a review on Amazon or Goodreads. I would appreciate it.

Thank you!

Other books published by Ralston Store Publishing:

Time Travel Sweet Romance
Cowgirls in Time Series by Erica Einhorn
A Chill Wind
Wind Beneath My Wings
Against the Wind
The Healing Wind
Ride Like the Wind
Wind of Change
The Way the Wind Blows

Rutledge Historical Society Cozy Mysteries
Message for Murder
Death over Divorce
Kousins Kan't Kill
Rogues to Riches
Secrets for Sale
Lady Smith Lady

Children's Books
Sparkles the Unicorn and Kindness
Cooper's Smile
The Little Unicorn Who Could
Do Bears Poop in the Woods?
Can Pigs Fly?
Why Do Puppy Dogs Have Cold Noses?
The Invisible Lion
La Petite Licorne Qui Pouvait
Das Kleine Einhorn Was Es Kann
The Little Unicorn Who Could Coloring Book
Do Bears Poop in the Woods? Coloring Book

Caregiving
The Journey that Matters by Jodie Lightener

Suspense
Darkness in the Light by J.K. Lincoln

India
Not My Guru by Parvati Hill

Women's Fiction/Reincarnation
Two Lifetimes, One Love by Thea Thaxton

Yoga Books
Bathroom Yoga
Airplane Yoga
Wheelchair Yoga
Essential Yoga on Horseback
Exercises for Therapeutic Riding

www.ingramcontent.com/pod-product-compliance
Lightning Source LLC
LaVergne TN
LVHW042349060326
832902LV00006B/484